Paul A. Davies · Carolyn Graham

Zabadoo!

Class Book 1

Contents

GW00692013

OXFORD

1 Listen, point and repeat.

2 Listen, point and repeat.

jeans   hamburger   tennis   Internet   computer   stop

3 Say the chant.

1, 2, 3, 4, 5 marbles.
How many more?
6, 7, 8, 9, 10.
Pick the marbles up again!

4 Listen, point and repeat. How many marbles?

one two three four five

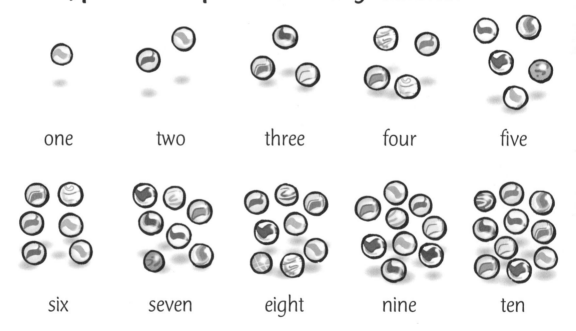

six seven eight nine ten

I'm Zabadoo!

6 Sing the song.

One head, two shoulders,
One mouth, two shoulders,
One nose, two shoulders,
How many toes? Ten toes!

Two eyes, two shoulders,
Two ears, two shoulders,
Two knees, two shoulders,
How many toes? Ten toes!

Read. Tick (✔) or cross (✘).

1	one + three = four	✔
2	seven - three = two	
3	five + three = eight	
4	six + two = nine	
5	ten - four = six	

1+3=4?

 Make a magic lamp. Play the game.

You need

   pages 93 and 95

1

Three?

2

Yes!

1 Say the chant.

Open your bag and look!
A rubber, a ruler,
A pencil, a pen,
And a book!

Open your bag and look!
A pencil, a pen,
And a book!

Open your bag and look!
A book!

Listen, point and repeat.

1 a rubber	2 a ruler	3 a pencil
4 a pen	5 a book	6 a bag

 Listen and circle.

5 **Look and write.**

Pen, pen, write again!

1

a <u>p e n c i l</u>

2

a _ _ _

3

a _ _ _ _ _

4

a _ _ _ _ _ _

5

a _ _ _ _ _ _

6

a _ _ _

6 Play

Zabadoo says...

1 Stand up!

2 Sit down!

3 Put your hand up!

4 Put your hand down!

7 Listen and act.

1 What's this? It's a book.

2 What's this? It's a pen.

3 What's this? It's my homework!

8 Listen, point and repeat.

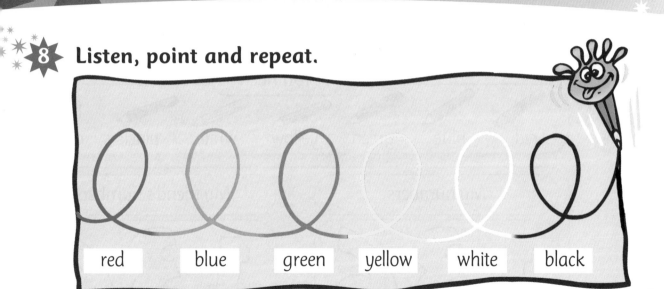

| red | blue | green | yellow | white | black |

9 Look. Tick (✔) or cross (✖).

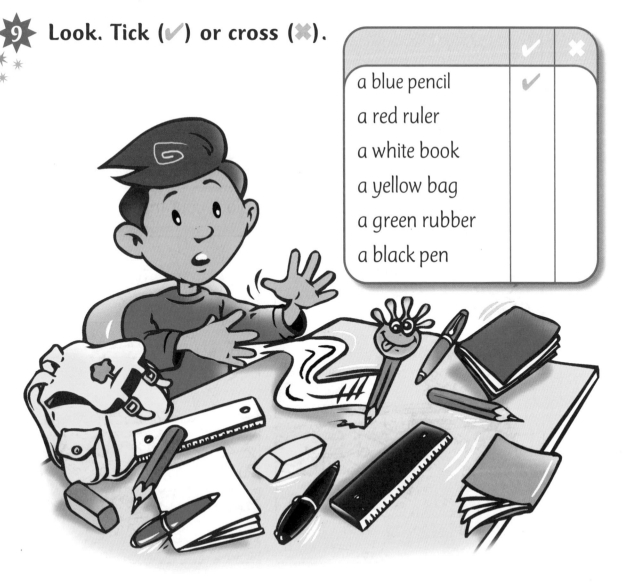

	✔	✖
a blue pencil	✔	
a red ruler		
a white book		
a yellow bag		
a green rubber		
a black pen		

10 Play the game.

You need

red   blue   green   yellow   white   black   a dice

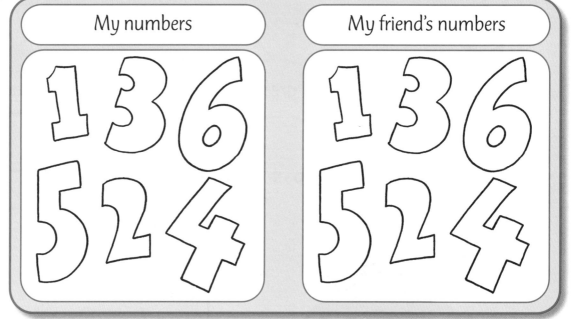

My numbers

1 3 6
5 2 4

My friend's numbers

1 3 6
5 2 4

Colour your numbers. Play and colour your friend's numbers.

Four. Is it red?

Yes!

Two. Is it blue?

No! My turn.

11 Sing the song.

Hi, how are you?
I'm fine, thank you.

Hi, how are you?
I'm fine, thank you.

Hi, how are you?
I'm fine. How are you?
I'm fine, thank you. I'm fine.

12 Circle and tick (✔).

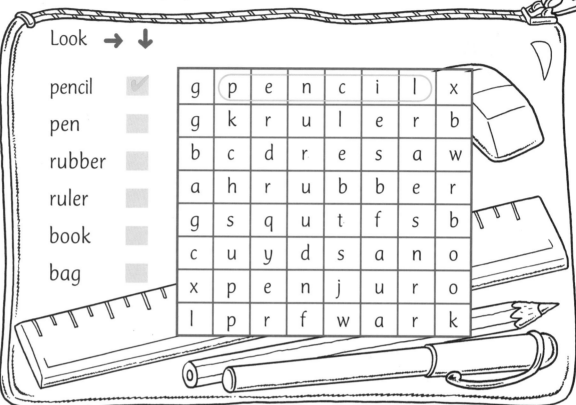

Look → ↓

g	p	e	n	c	i	l	x
g	k	r	u	l	e	r	b
b	c	d	r	e	s	a	w
a	h	r	u	b	b	e	r
g	s	q	u	t	f	s	b
c	u	y	d	s	a	n	o
x	p	e	n	j	u	r	o
l	p	r	f	w	a	r	k

pencil ✔

pen ☐

rubber ☐

ruler ☐

book ☐

bag ☐

13 Make a picture.

My pencil case

a red ruler

1 2 3 4 5 6 7 8 9 10

a green pen   a yellow rubber

Laura

Time for fun!

A Look and write.

I'm Leo. I'm ten.

_____

_____

B Read and colour.

one = blue	two = green	three = yellow
four = red	five = black	six = white

C Count and write. Then colour.

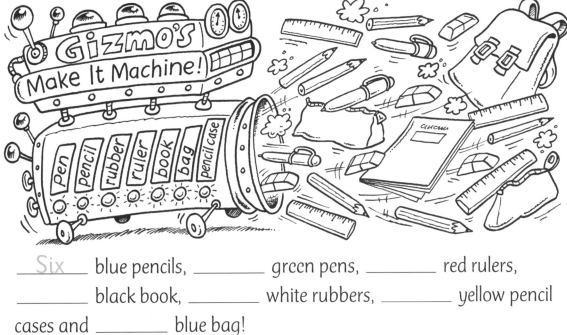

___Six___ blue pencils, _____ green pens, _____ red rulers, _____ black book, _____ white rubbers, _____ yellow pencil cases and _____ blue bag!

Zabadoo, Zabadee!
Can you answer 1, 2, 3?

Zabadee, Zabadoo!
Can you do 1 and 2?

1 What's your name?

2 How old are you?

3 What's this?

1 Say a chant.

2 Say six colours.

  Well done!

Message: Hi! I'm Will. Welcome to my website! Look at my school friends...

Will's Website

- **school**
- clothes
- **at home**
- food
- **favourite things**

Start
View
Choose
End

Listen and number.

a

b

c

1 the lollipop lady

d

e

f

Match and write.

1 the lollipop lady
2 the playground
3 assembly
4 my teacher
5 sports day
6 my class

Start
View
Choose
End

 Say the chant.

I put on my socks,
I put on my shoes,
I put on my shirt,
And my trousers, too.

I put on my jacket,
I put on my hat,
Look! I'm a clown!
And who are you?

Listen, point and repeat. Then play.

a hat	a shirt	a jacket
a T-shirt	a skirt	trousers
shorts	socks	shoes

 Listen and colour.

a hat

♪♪ I'm a pop star ...

a T-shirt

a skirt

a jacket

socks

shoes

Read, colour and write.

1  Change to blue!

blue s h o e s

2  Change to green!

a green s _ _ _ _ _

3  Change to red!

red t _ _ _ _ _ _ _ _

4  Change to yellow!

a yellow s _ _ _ _ _ _

6 Play

1	2	3
Turn around!	Pick up a pencil!	Put down the pencil!

7 Listen and act.

Gizmo and Hoot

1. Shh! I'm wearing a green tracksuit and a green hat.

2. Hello, Gizmo.

3. Oh. I'm wearing red shoes!

Read and colour.

 1

I'm a footballer!
I'm wearing a yellow
T-shirt, blue shorts
and white socks.

 2

I'm a dancer! I'm
wearing a red dress
and black shoes.

Listen, point and repeat.

orange   purple   pink   grey   brown

 Play the game.

28

Sing the song.

She's a pop star. Wow!
She's wearing green jeans.
She's a pop star. Wow!
She's wearing green jeans.
She's wearing green socks.
She's wearing green shoes.
She's a pop star. Wow!
She's wearing green.

He's a pirate. Wow!
He's wearing black jeans.
He's a pirate. Wow!
He's wearing black jeans.
He's wearing black socks.
He's wearing black shoes.
He's a pirate. Wow!
He's wearing black.

12 **Colour.**

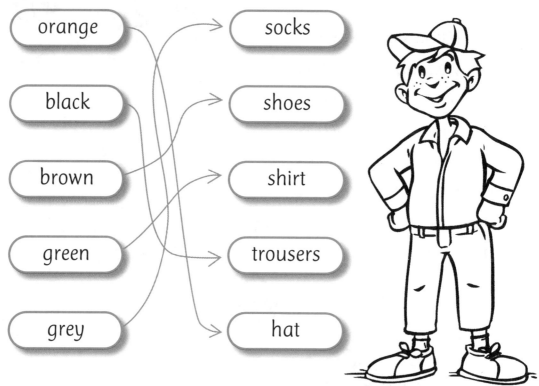

orange	socks
black	shoes
brown	shirt
green	trousers
grey	hat

13 **Make a picture.**

I'm wearing blue shorts and a pink T-shirt.

Laura

Bob the fish and Olly the octopus Snapper the crab

Time for fun!

A **Write and colour.**

Gizmo's Mix It Machine!

| black | white | red | blue | yellow |

brown

B **Circle and tick (✔).**

Look → ↓

hat
jacket
shirt
trousers
dress
shoes ✔
socks
shorts
T-shirt
skirt
tracksuit

s	h	t	a	s	h	o	e	s	t
t	s	r	c	j	a	s	d	h	r
h	h	a	k	a	j	a	s	o	o
a	i	s	o	c	k	s	k	r	u
t	r	a	c	k	s	u	i	t	s
r	t	d	r	e	s	s	r	s	e
s	j	e	c	t	u	i	t	h	r
T	-	s	h	i	r	t	e	s	s

Write and colour.

one = <u>blue</u>
two = _____
three = _____
four = _____
five = _____
six = _____

I'm wearing <u>a</u>
<u>blue hat,</u>
_____
_____
_____
_____
_____
_____
_____

Zabadee, Zabadoo!
Can you answer 1 and 2?

Zabadoo, Zabadee!
Can you do 1, 2, 3?

1 What are you
   wearing?

2 What colour are
   your shoes?

1 Say 11 colours.

2 Sing a song.

3 Turn around.

Well done!

Message: Hi! Look at these clothes!

Will's Website

- Start
- View
- Choose
- End

- school
- **clothes**
- at home
- food
- favourite things

Listen and number.

b

a

c

Search Back Forward Stop Home Favourites

d

1 <u>a fireman</u>

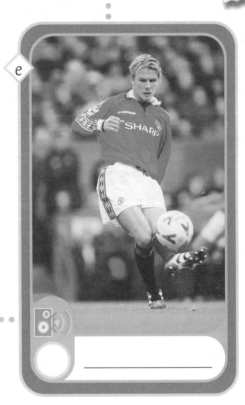

e

_____

f

_____

Match and write.

1 a fireman

2 a nurse

3 I'm a cub scout!

4 a footballer

5 a policewoman

6 a guard

Start
View
Choose
End

 Say the chant.

Pull, pull my grandad's shoe!
Me and my mum,
And my sister, too.

Pull, pull my grandad's shoe!
My dad and my brother,
And my grandma, too.

One … two … three … Help!

2 Listen, point and number.

Hide and seek

4 **Listen, point and say.**

dining room   living room   bathroom   kitchen   bedroom

5 **Look and write.**

Where's Zabadoo?   He's in the _____.
Where's Leo?   He's in the _____.
Where's Laura?   She's in the _____.

6 **Play**

Zabadoo says...

1 Close your eyes!

2 Open your eyes!

3 Count to ten!

7 **Listen and act.**

1 The Look Out! Machine

Where's your brother?

2 In the kitchen. Look!

brother

Where's your mum?

3 Look Out! Machine

mum

Oh no! In my bedroom!

Listen, read and colour.

Listen, point and repeat.

Zabadoo   Leo   Laura   Tim   Jack   Emma

10 Play the game.

11 **Sing the song.**

Where's Grandad?
Climbing up the stairs.
Where's Grandad?
Climbing up the stairs.
Slowly, slowly,
Climbing up the stairs.
Grandad's climbing up the stairs. (*Puff, puff, puff!*)

Where's Grandma?
Running down the stairs.
Where's Grandma?
Running down the stairs.
Quickly, quickly,
Running down the stairs.
Grandma's running down the stairs. (*Oops!*)

12 **Listen and join the dots.**

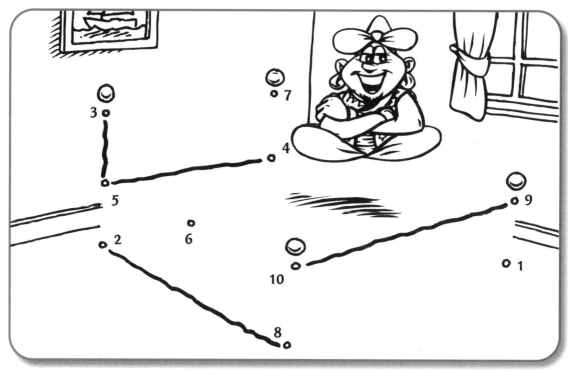

Where's Zabadoo?   In the _____ .

 13 **Make a picture.**

My family and friends

My mum

My brother, Tim

My friend, Laura

Leo

Time for fun!

A Write.

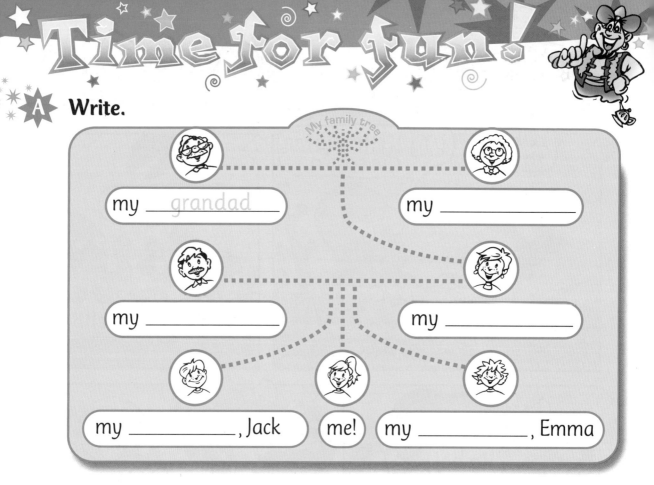

my __grandad__

my _____

my _____

my _____

my _____, Jack

me!

my _____, Emma

My family tree

B Draw and write.

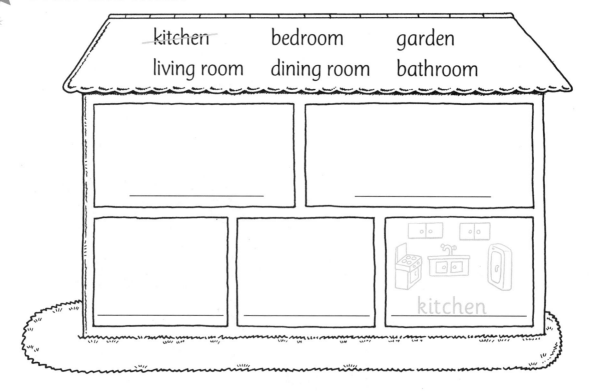

kitchen   bedroom   garden

living room   dining room   bathroom

_____   _____

_____   _____   kitchen

C **Write. Then draw Gizmo and Hoot.**

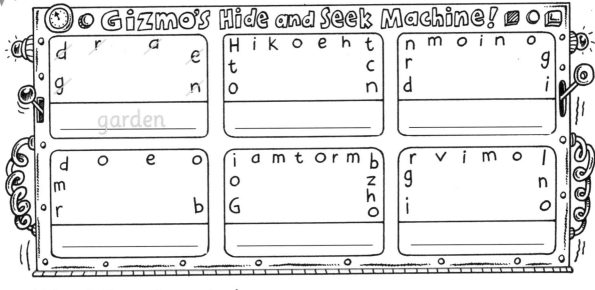

Gizmo's Hide and Seek Machine!

d r a e	H i k o e h t	n m o i n o
d g n	t c o n c	r d g i
garden	_____	_____

d o e o	i a m t o r m b	r v i m o l
m r b	o G z h o	g i n o
_____	_____	_____

Where's Gizmo?   In the _____.

Where's Hoot?   In the _____.

Zabadee, Zabadoo!
Can you answer 1 and 2?

Zabadoo, Zabadee!
Can you do 1, 2, 3?

1 Who's your friend?

2 What's your mum's name?

1 Say five rooms.

2 Count to ten.

3 Close your eyes.

Well done!

Message: Hi! Look at my house, family and friends!

Will's Website

Start

View

Choose

End

- school
- clothes
- **at home**
- food
- favourite things

Listen and number.

a

b

c

Search Back Forward Stop Home Favourites

_____

e

_____

f

_____

Match and write.

1 my bedroom
2 my family
3 my best friend, Tom
4 my house
5 my dog, Goldie
6 my garden

Start
View
Choose
End

 Say the chant.

Can I have some pasta?
Can I have some rice?
Can I have some chicken?
Mmmm! Very nice!

Can I have some salad?
Can I have some cheese?
Can I have some pizza?
Mmmm! More, please!

2 Listen and number.

chicken

rice

pizza

cheese

pasta

salad

3 Read and draw.

Pizza and salad. My favourite food!

5 **Match.**

Zabadoo's café
Menu

pizza
pasta
fish
chicken
chips
rice
salad
cheese
ice-cream

6 **Listen and act.**

Pasta and salad, please.

OK.

Here you are!

Thank you!

53

7 Play

Zabadoo says...

1 Point to the board!

2 Point to the door!

3 Point to the window!

4 Point to the floor!

8 Listen and act.

Gizmo and Hoot

1 Fantastic Food Factory

pizza salad ice-cream chips

Mmmm! Pizza!

I don't like pizza.

2 Mmmm! Salad.

I don't like salad.

3 Mmmm! I like ice-cream and chips.

9 **Look and write.**

I like rice.

I don't like chicken.

10 **Draw and write.**

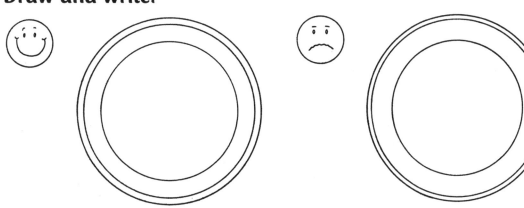

I like _____.   I don't like _____.

11 Listen. Ask and answer.

Do you like...?	Me ✓ or X	My friend ✓ or X

12 Listen. Ask and answer.

Sing the song.

Daddy, Daddy, can I have some ice-cream?
Daddy, Daddy, can I have some ice-cream?

Please, Daddy! Can I have some ice-cream?
Can I have some ice-cream?

    Yes, you can.

Thank you, Daddy, I love ice-cream.
Thank you, Daddy, I love ice-cream.

I love ice-cream, I love ice-cream.
Can I have some ice-cream?

    Yes, you can.

14 Read and match.

1 I like fish.
I don't like chips.

a

2 I like pizza.
I don't like salad.

b

3 I like chicken.
I don't like pizza.

c

4 I like chips.
I don't like chicken.

d

15 Make a picture.

Menu
My Super Sandwich
pizza and ice-cream
Zabadoo

A **Draw and write.**

~~phics~~	nekhicc	ecaemi-cr
dalsa	icre	izapz
tasap	shfi	seceeh

GIZMO's
FANTASTIC FOOD FACTORY
MENU

chips

B Do the puzzle.

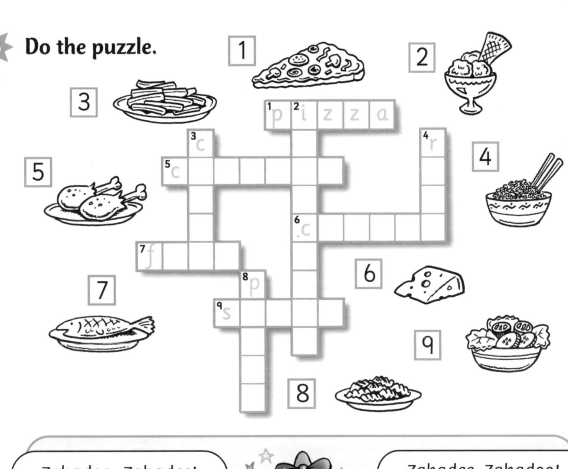

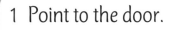

Zabadoo, Zabadee!
Can you answer 1, 2, 3?

Zabadee, Zabadoo!
Can you do 1 and 2?

1 Are you hungry?

2 Do you like fish?

3 What's your favourite food?

1 Point to the door.

2 Point to your friend.

Well done!

Message: Hi! Look at this food!

Will's Website

1

- school
- at home
- **food**
- favourite things

Listen and number.

b

a

c

_____

e

_____

f

_____

Match and write.

1 my favourite meal

2 my birthday cake

3 ice-cream

4 Sunday lunch

5 school dinner

6 English breakfast

Start

View

Choose

End

1 Say the chant.

A pink computer,
And a red guitar,
A big, yellow football,
And a little, orange car,
A green television,
And a big, blue kite ...
– What's your favourite colour?
– Er ... It's white!

2 **Listen and match. Then colour.**

What's that?

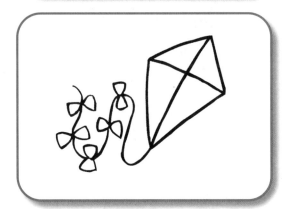

4 **Read, draw and colour.**

a red and blue kite

a brown and black football

a brown and blue guitar

a red and black car

Blue, black, go back!

5 Play

Zabadoo says...

1 Jump!

2 Hop!

3 Stamp your feet!

4 Nod your head!

6 Listen and act.

I've got a bike, a guitar and a _____.

①

I've got a bag, a television and a _____.

②

I've got a kite, a car and a _____.

③

I've got a skateboard, a computer and a _____.

④

8 **Make cards.**

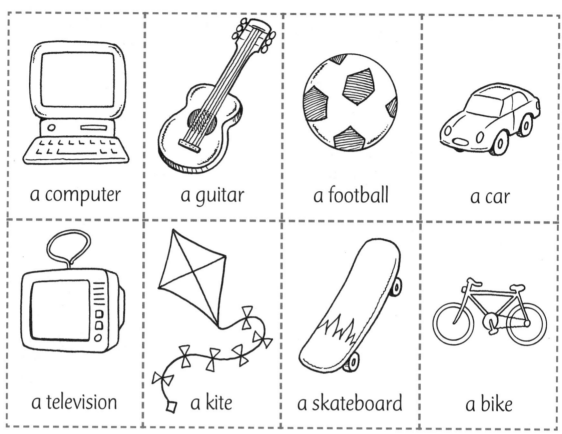

a computer	a guitar	a football	a car
a television	a kite	a skateboard	a bike

9 **Play the game.**

Have you got a bike?

No.

Have you got a television?

Yes. Here you are.

10 Sing the song.

My favourite colour is red.
My favourite colour is blue.
My favourite colour is purple.
Oh, I love purple too!

My favourite colour is green.
My favourite colour is blue.
My favourite colour is yellow.
Oh, I love yellow too!

11 **Do the puzzle.**

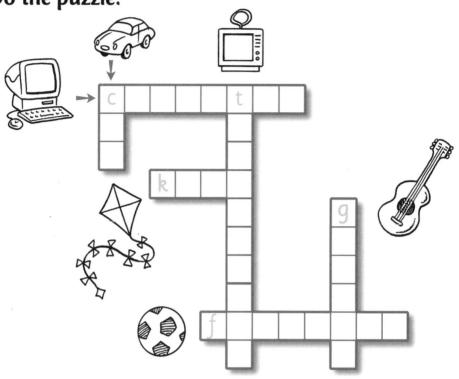

12 **Make a picture.**

72

73

A Write.

Gizmo's Word Sorter

~~red~~ ~~hat~~ ~~kite~~ ~~fish~~ ~~pencil~~ ~~kitchen~~ living room
shirt computer chips green rubber jacket
guitar yellow ruler pizza bedroom pasta skirt
pen football bathroom blue dress car rice
black shorts television white garden cheese
brown chicken socks purple bag skateboard
ice-cream shoes orange salad bike pink
book tracksuit sandwich pencil case trousers
dining room jeans grey

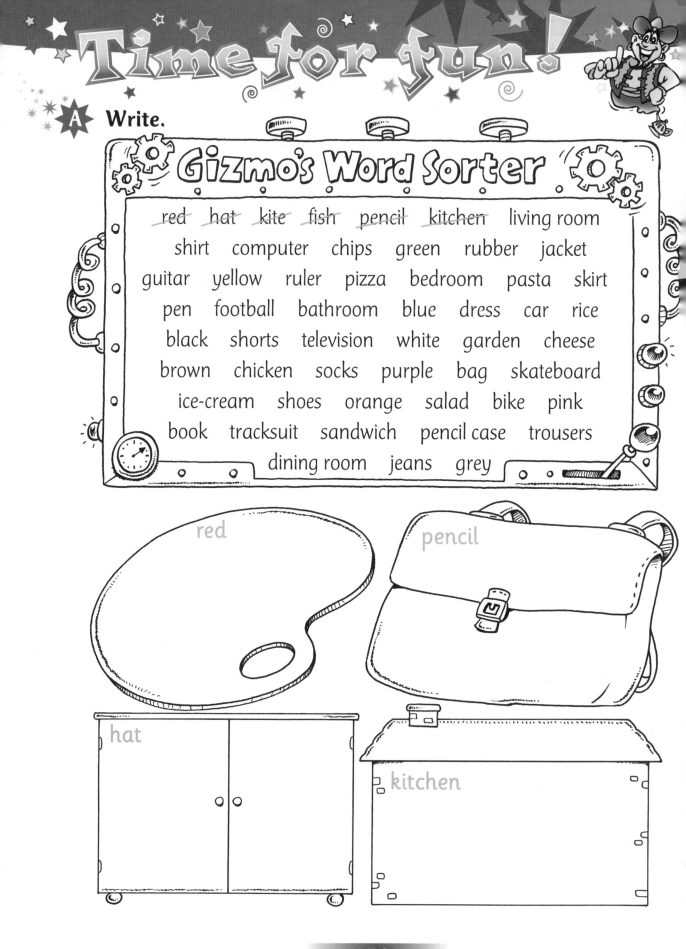

red

pencil

hat

kitchen

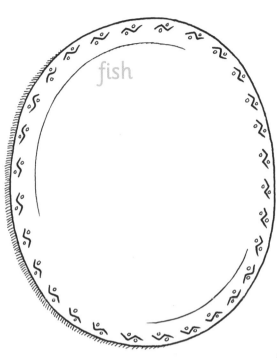

fish

The Toy Shop

kite

Zabadoo, Zabadee!
Can you answer 1, 2, 3?

Zabadee, Zabadoo!
Can you do 1 and 2?

1 Have you got
   a football?

2 What's your
   favourite toy?

3 What's your
   favourite colour?

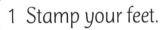

1 Stamp your feet.

2 Say six toys.

Well done!

75

Message: Hi! Look at my favourite things!

Will's Website

Start
View
Choose
End

- school
- clothes
- at home
- food
- **favourite things**

Listen and number.

b

a

c

Search Back Forward Stop Home Favourites

d

_____

e

_____

_____

f

_____

_____

Match and write.

1 my favourite day
2 my favourite place
3 my favourite festival
4 my favourite football team
5 my favourite pop star
6 my favourite lesson

Start
View
Choose
End

Little Red Ridinghood

Listen and act.

Scene 1   *Little Red Ridinghood is going to visit her grandma.*

Red Ridinghood: It's Grandma's birthday! Daddy, can I have some chocolates?

All and Daddy: ♫ *Daddy, Daddy, can I have some chocolates?*

Red Ridinghood: Thank you, Daddy. Mmm. Chocolates for Grandma!

Daddy: Goodbye. And look out for the wolf!

Red Ridinghood: Yes, Daddy. See you later!

Scene 2   *In the forest.*

Red Ridinghood: Look! Flowers for Grandma!

Trees: ♫ *My favourite colour is red*

Bird 1:   A red flower for Grandma.

Bird 2:   A yellow flower for Grandma.

Bird 3:   A purple flower for Grandma.

Bird 4:   A pink flower for Grandma.

Wolf: Ha, ha! Look! My favourite food!

Scene 3

Trees:

At Grandma and Grandad's house.
🎵 Where's Grandad?
(Knock, knock at the door.)

Birds:

🎵 Where's Grandma?

Grandma: Who is it?

Wolf: Little Red Ridinghood!

Grandma: Come in.

Wolf: Ha, ha!

Scene 4

Later. (Knock, knock at the door.)

Wolf: Who is it?

Red Ridinghood: Little Red Ridinghood!

Wolf: Come in.

Trees: He's a wolf! Look out!

Birds: He's wearing Grandma's clothes!

Red Ridinghood: Grandma, what big eyes!

Wolf: All the better to see you!

Red Ridinghood: Grandma, what big ears!

Wolf: All the better to hear you!

Red Ridinghood: Grandma, what big teeth!

Wolf: All the better to eat you!!!

Red Ridinghood: Help!

Grandad: It's OK. I'm here!

Wolf: Help!

Red Ridinghood: Where's Grandma?

Grandma: I'm here. ... Thank you!

Red Ridinghood: Happy birthday, Grandma!

Do the birthday chant.

Boys and girls,
Boys and girls,
When's your birthday?
Please stand up!

January, February,
March, April,
May, June,
July, August,
September, October,
November, December!

Boys and girls,
Boys and girls,
When's your birthday?
Please sit down!

January, February ...
November, December!

Make a class calendar.

Play 'Pass the parcel'.

1. Sing a song!
2. Count to ten!
3. Stand up!
4. Write your name!
5. Say a colour!
6. Draw your teacher!
7. Say a chant!
8. How old are you?
9. When's your birthday?
10. You're Zabadoo!

Pass the parcel and count.

Stop, read and do.

Sing the song.

Black cat, witch's hat,
Happy Halloween!

Long, white witch's hair,
Happy Halloween!

Pumpkin lantern, cat's eyes,
Happy Halloween!

Black and white, orange and green,
These are the colours of Halloween.
Black and white, orange and green,
Happy Halloween!

Happy Halloween

Make a Halloween mask.

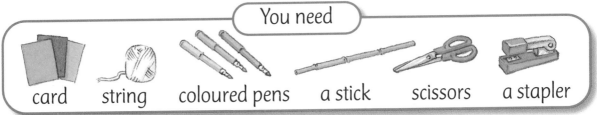

You need

card string coloured pens a stick scissors a stapler

I'm a black cat!

I'm a pumpkin!

I'm a witch!

It's Christmas!

Sing the song.

O Christmas tree, O Christmas tree,
How lovely are your branches!
O Christmas tree, O Christmas tree,
How lovely are your branches!

In summer sun or winter snow,
A coat of green you always show.
O Christmas tree, O Christmas tree,
How lovely are your branches!

Make and decorate a Christmas tree.

You need

card   paper   a box   a cardboard tube

scissors   glue   glitter   cotton wool   ribbon

a star   an angel

a bell   a snowball

a present   a cracker

Listen and act.

It's **Father Christmas!**

Scene 1   It's Christmas. Leo, Laura and their schoolfriends are going to a fancy dress party at school.

Leo:	I'm Leo!
Laura:	And I'm Laura.
Friends:	Come on! Let's go!
All:	♫ Jingle bells, jingle bells, jingle all the way, Oh what fun it is to ride, in a one-horse open sleigh!

Scene 2   At the party.

Miss Green:	Hello, everyone!
Chorus:	♫ Hi, how are you?
All:	Look at the Christmas tree!
Laura:	A star!
Friend 1:	An angel!
Katy:	A bell!
Leo:	A snowball!
Friend 2:	A present!
Tom:	A cracker!
Chorus:	♫ O Christmas tree

Scene 3

It's time for the fancy dress prizes.

Miss Green: Third prize. Who are you?

Katy: I'm a pop star.

Friends: It's Katy!

Chorus: 🎵 *She's a pop star*

Miss Green: Second prize. Who are you?

Tom: I'm a pirate.

Friends: It's Tom!

Chorus: 🎵 *He's a pirate*

Miss Green: First prize. Who are you?

Father Christmas: I'm Father Christmas.

Leo and Laura: Are you Zabadoo?

Father Christmas: Ouch! No! I'm Father Christmas!

Friends: It *is* Father Christmas!

Father Christmas: Yes! And here are your presents!

All: Thank you, Father Christmas!

Scene 4

It's time to go home.

Father Christmas: Goodbye, everyone! Merry Christmas!

All: Goodbye, Father Christmas!
And Merry Christmas, everyone!

All: 🎵 *We wish you a Merry Christmas,*
We wish you a Merry Christmas,
We wish you a Merry Christmas,
And a Happy New Year!

 Sing the song.

Easter Bunny,
Easter eggs,
On Easter Sunday morning.

Easter Bunny,
Easter eggs,
On Easter Sunday morning.

Easter baskets,
Pink and blue.
One for me,
And one for you.

Easter baskets,
Pink and blue,
On Easter Sunday morning.

Make an Easter card.

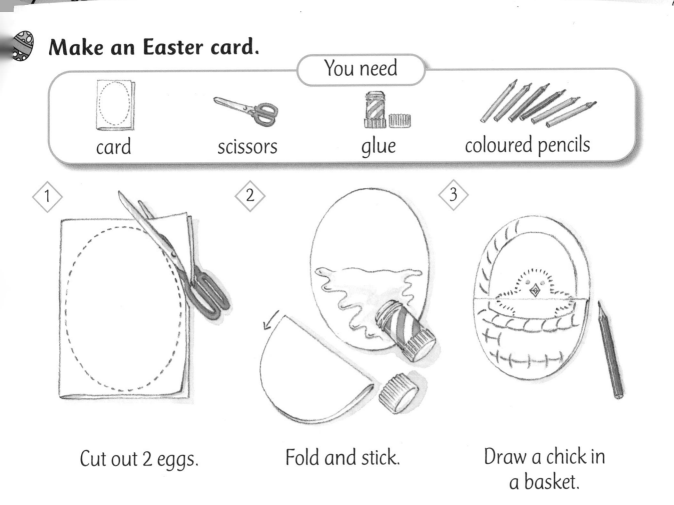

You need

card   scissors   glue   coloured pencils

1 Cut out 2 eggs.

2 Fold and stick.

3 Draw a chick in a basket.

4 Write and decorate.

5 Close, write and decorate.

Wordlist

Unit 1

a
again
computer
ear
eight
eye
five
four
hamburger
head
Hello!/Hi!
How many more?
How old are you?
I'm (Leo).
I'm (nine).
Internet
jeans
knee
lamp
magic
marble
mouth
Mrs
my
nine
nose
one
pick up
seven
shoulder
six
stop
ten
tennis
the
three
toe
two
What's this?
What's your name?
Yes

Unit 2

and
assembly
bag
black
blue
book
class
Come on!
crab
fish
friend
green
hand
Here's ...
homework
How are you?
I'm fine.
Is it (red)?
It's a ...
Leo's
lollipop lady
look
Look out!
Miss
My turn.
name
new
No
octopus
open
pen
pencil
pencil case
playground
please
put down
put up
Quick!
red
rubber
ruler
school
Sit down!
Sorry!
spell
sports day
Stand up!
teacher
Thank you.
Time for ...
website
Well done!
white
write
yellow
your
You're late.

Unit 3

brown
change
clothes
clown
Come back!
cub scout
dancer
dress
fireman
footballer
grey
guard
hat
he
Help!
here
hide
I'm wearing ...
jacket
number
nurse
orange
pink
pirate
policewoman
pop star
princess
purple
put on
she
shirt
shoes
shorts
skirt
socks
Thanks.
these
this
too
tracksuit
trousers
T-shirt
turn around
Who are you?

Unit 4
at home
bathroom
bedroom
best
big
brother
Christmas
climb up
close
Coming!
count
dad
dog
family
find
for
garden
grandad
grandma
hide and seek
house
kitchen
Let's play …
little
living room
me
mum
pull
quickly
room
run down
sister
slowly
stairs
to
Where's …?
Who's …?

Unit 5
birthday cake
board
Can I have …?
cheese
chicken
chips
door
Do you like …?
English breakfast

favourite
floor
food
Here you are!
ice-cream
I like/I don't like …
I love …
I'm hungry.
meal
point
rice
salad
school dinner
seaweed
See you later.
some
still
Sunday lunch
Very nice!
window
wish for

Unit 6
bike
car
Come down!
day
fantastic
festival
football
Go back!
goodbye
guitar
Have you got…?
hop
I've got …
jump
kite
lesson
nod (your head)
over there
place
skateboard
stamp (your feet)
team
television
things
toy

Little Red Ridinghood
eat
flower
hear
see
teeth
wolf

It's your birthday!
April
August
boy
calendar
December
February
girl
January
July
June
March
May
November
October
September
When?

It's Halloween!
cat
pumpkin
witch

It's Christmas!
branch
snow
coat
summer
sun
winter

It's Father Christmas!
first
party
prize
second
sleigh
third

It's Easter!
basket
bunny
egg

OXFORD
UNIVERSITY PRESS

Great Clarendon Street, Oxford OX2 6DP

Oxford University Press is a department of the University of Oxford.
It furthers the University's objective of excellence in research, scholarship,
and education by publishing worldwide in

Oxford New York

Auckland Cape Town Dar es Salaam Hong Kong Karachi
Kuala Lumpur Madrid Melbourne Mexico City Nairobi
New Delhi Shanghai Taipei Toronto

With offices in

Argentina Austria Brazil Chile Czech Republic France Greece
Guatemala Hungary Italy Japan Poland Portugal Singapore
South Korea Switzerland Thailand Turkey Ukraine Vietnam

OXFORD and OXFORD ENGLISH are registered trade marks of
Oxford University Press in the UK and in certain other countries

ACKNOWLEDGEMENTS

Main Artists: Leo and Laura artwork by Nick Diggory, Gizmo and Hoot
artwork by Garry Davies, Bob and Olly cartoon by Renée Mansfield

Other Artists: Kelly Harrison pp 29, 57, 80, 81; Claire Mumford pp 15, 71, 82,
83, 88, 89; Mark Ruffle pp 16, 30, 41, 44, 58, 72; Adam Stower pp 43, 78, 79

Commissioned Photography by: Haddon Davies pp 20 (computer, playground
games, assembly), 21 (class, teacher), 34 (computer, scouts), 48 (computer,
bike, swingball, dog), 49 (picnic, bedroom, house), 62 (computer), 63
(Sunday lunch, birthday cake), 76 (computer, art lesson), 77 (skateboard,
Halloween, pop star)

The publishers would like to thank the following for permission to reproduce
photographs: Anthony Blake Photo Library p 62 (English breakfast/Kieran
Scott); Bubbles Photo Library p 20 (lollipop lady/Jennie Woodcock); Food
Features p 63 (fish & chips); Photofusion pp 34 (guard/Vania Coimbra, nurse
with patient/Julia Martin), 35 (fireman/Paul Doyle), 62 (ice cream van/
Christa Stadtler, school dinner/Julia Martin); Popperfoto pp 35 (David
Beckham, police/Jeff J Mitchell/Reuters), 76 (Manchester United); Janine
Wiedel p 21 (sports day)

My magic lamp

Name

Make a magic lamp.

1 Fold line **A–B**.

2 Cut out circle. Open.

3 Fold line **C–D**.

4 Cut flap. Open.

5 Make a hole.

6 Write your name. Colour and decorate your lamp.

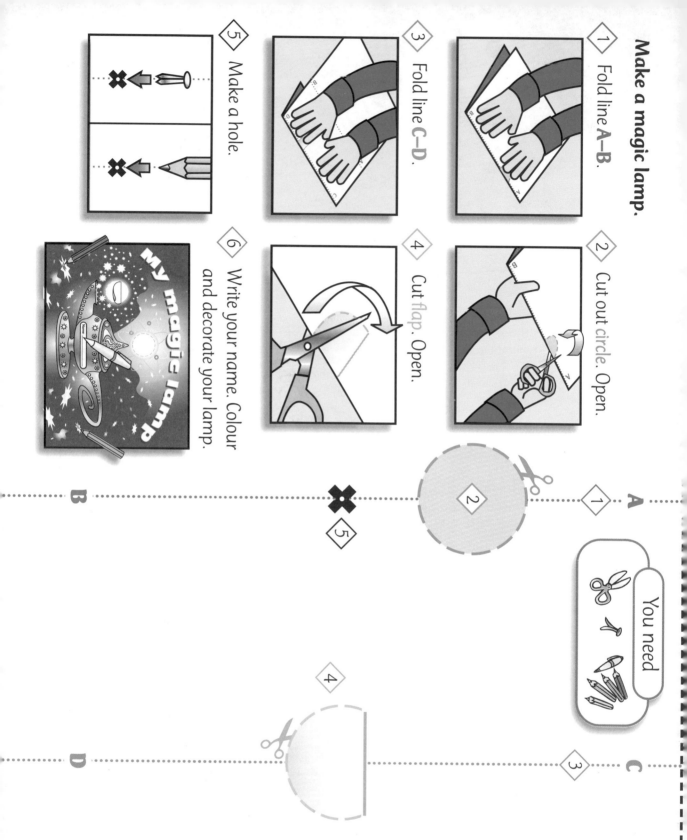

MY magic lamp

You need

A

B

C

D

1

2

3

4

5

Make the disc for your magic lamp.

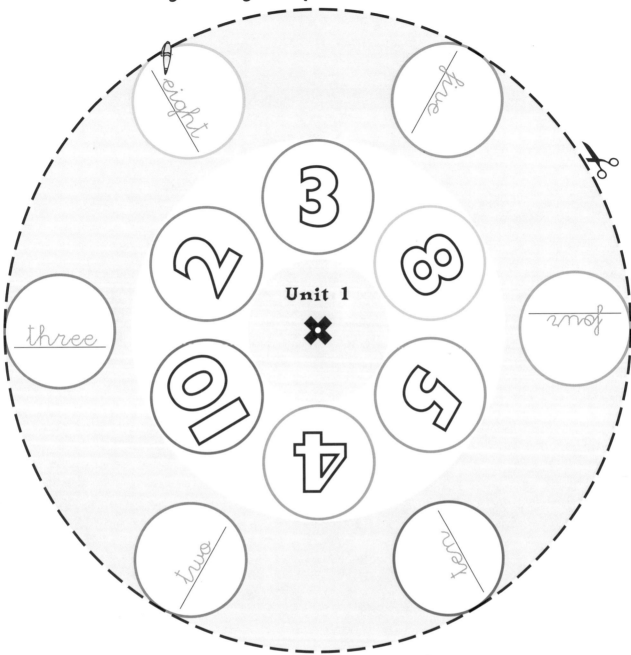

eight

five

3

2

Unit 1

8

three

four

10

5

4

two

ten

① Cut out the disc.

② Make a hole.

③ Trace the words. Colour the numbers.

You need

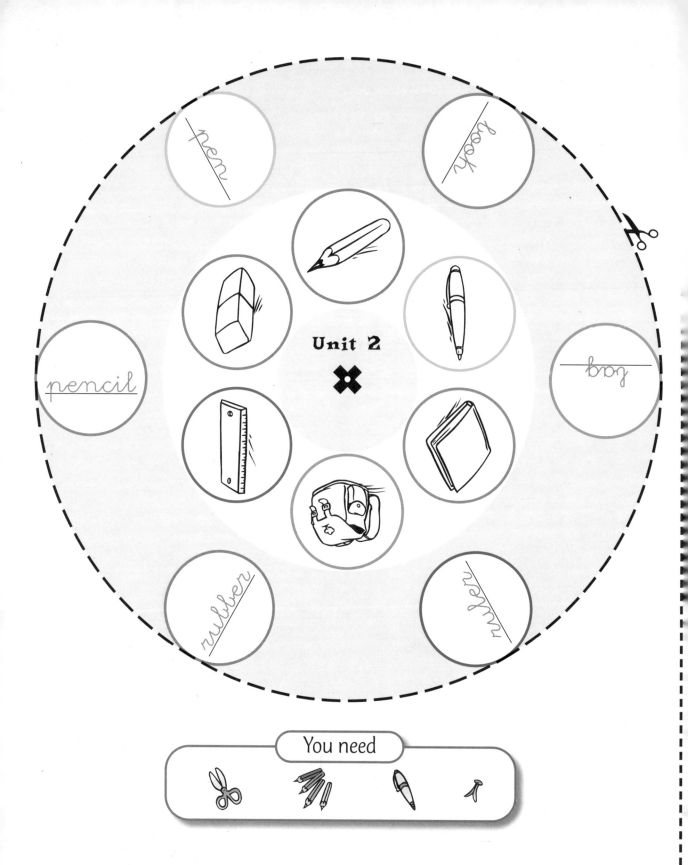

Unit 2

pen

book

pencil

bag

rubber

ruler

You need